Expect more from your crochet!

I0884179

These four easy designs have all the **plush comfort** you crave, plus an unexpected bonus. Two of the wraps have convenient string ties while the Not-So-Granny Square Wrap has a deep, fuzzy fringe that sways in the lightest breeze. And for **refreshing originality**, the thick fabric of the Artistic Wrap is interspersed with the knotted ends of scrap yarns. Congratulate yourself on finding four charming crochet fashions that are not only **completely cozy**, but also **completely unique!**

ARTISTIC WRAP

Shown on Back Cover.

INTERMEDIATE

Finished Size: Adult

MATERIALS

BULKY 5

Bulky Weight Yarn
[6 ounces, 185 yards
(170 grams, 167 meters) per skein]:
Main Color - 4 skeins
"Raggy ball" - approximately 24 ounces
Crochet hook, size K (6.5 mm) **or** size needed for gauge

Note: To make a "raggy ball" cut scrap yarn in various lengths, anywhere from 10-30" (25.5-76 cm). This can be done quickly by holding several strands together, wrapping them around a book or piece of cardboard, then cut yarn at the bottom (as though you are making fringe). Tie random strands together with one overhand knot; do **not** trim ends. Wind in a ball as you go. Feel free to use many different colors and weights of yarn, including novelty yarns. When you have a ball about the size of a melon, **begin Poncho holding one strand of your raggy ball and one strand of Bulky Weight yarn together as one**. If you run out of raggy ball, make another small raggy ball and add to the end of your first ball. As you crochet your Poncho, let the knot ends land where they will to add texture and interest.

GAUGE: With double strand of yarn,
8 dc and 5 rows = 4" (10 cm)

Gauge Swatch: 4" (10 cm) square
With double strand of yarn, ch 10.
Row 1: Dc in fourth ch from hook **(3 skipped chs count as first dc)** and in each ch across: 8 dc.
Rows 2-5: Ch 3 **(counts as first dc)**, turn; dc in next dc and in each dc across.
Finish off.

WRAP

Beginning at neckline with double strand of yarn, ch 52; being careful not to twist ch, join with slip st to form a ring.

Rnd 1 (Right side)**:** Ch 3 **(counts as first dc, now and throughout)**, dc in next 24 chs, (2 dc, ch 2, 2 dc) in next ch, dc in next 25 chs, (2 dc, ch 2, 2 dc) in last ch; join with slip st to first dc: 58 dc and 2 ch-2 sps.

Note: Loop a short piece of yarn around any stitch to mark Rnd 1 as **right** side.

Rnd 2: Ch 3, turn; dc in next 2 dc, (2 dc, ch 2, 2 dc) in next ch-2 sp, dc in next 29 dc, (2 dc, ch 2, 2 dc) in next ch-2 sp, dc in last 26 dc; join with slip st to first dc: 66 dc and 2 ch-2 sps.

Rnds 3-20: Ch 3, turn; ★ dc in next dc and in each dc across to next ch-2 sp, (2 dc, ch 2, 2 dc) in ch-2 sp; repeat from ★ once **more**, dc in next dc and in each dc across; join with slip st to first dc: 210 dc and 2 ch-2 sps.

Finish off.

Holding 4 strands of yarn together, each 20" (51 cm) long, add fringe evenly around bottom edge of Wrap ***(Figs. 8a & b, page 12)***.

JUST FOR ME

Shown on Front Cover.

EASY

Finished Size: Adult

MATERIALS

Bulky Weight Yarn (BULKY 5)
[6 ounces, 185 yards
(170 grams, 167 meters) per skein]:
3 skeins
Crochet hook, size K (6.5 mm) **or** size needed for gauge

GAUGE: 9 dc and 6 rows = 4" (10 cm)

Gauge Swatch: 4" (10 cm) square
Ch 11.
Row 1: Dc in fourth ch from hook **(3 skipped chs count as one dc)** and in each ch across: 9 dc.
Rows 2-6: Ch 3 **(counts as first dc)**, turn; dc in next dc and in each dc across.
Finish off.

STITCH GUIDE

BEGINNING DECREASE (uses first 2 dc)
YO, insert hook in **first** dc, YO and pull up a loop, YO and draw through 2 loops on hook, YO, insert hook in **next** dc, YO and pull up a loop, YO and draw through 2 loops on hook, YO and draw through all 3 loops on hook **(counts as one dc)**.
DECREASE (uses next 2 dc)
★ YO, insert hook in **next** dc, YO and pull up a loop, YO and draw through 2 loops on hook; repeat from ★ once **more**, YO and draw through all 3 loops on hook **(counts as one dc)**.

WRAP

Wrap is worked from side-to-side starting at one point and increasing every row (on one side only) toward center back, then decreasing every row (on one side only) and working to other point.

Row 1: Ch 3, 2 dc in third ch from hook: 2 dc.

Row 2 (Right side)**:** Ch 2, turn; dc in first dc, 2 dc in last dc: 3 dc.

Note: Loop a short piece of yarn around any stitch to mark Row 2 as **right** side.

Row 3: Ch 2, turn; 2 dc in first dc, dc in last 2 dc: 4 dc.

Row 4 (Increase row)**:** Ch 2, turn; dc in first dc and in each dc across to last dc, 2 dc in last dc: 5 dc.

Row 5 (Increase row)**:** Ch 2, turn; 2 dc in first dc, dc in next dc and in each dc across: 6 dc.

Rows 6-31: Repeat Rows 4 and 5, 13 times; at end of Row 31, finish off: 32 dc.

Row 32: Ch 50 (tie), with **right** side facing, join yarn with dc in first dc ***(see Joining With Dc, page 12)***; dc in next dc and in each dc across to last dc, 2 dc in last dc: 33 dc and one tie.

Row 33: Ch 2, turn; 2 dc in first dc, dc in next dc and in each dc across leaving tie unworked: 34 dc.

Rows 34-49: Repeat Rows 4 and 5, 8 times: 50 dc.

Row 50 (Decrease row)**:** Ch 2, turn; dc in first dc and in each dc across to last 2 dc, decrease: 49 dc.

Row 51 (Decrease row)**:** Ch 2, turn; work beginning decrease, dc in next dc and in each dc across: 48 dc.

Rows 52-66: Repeat Rows 50 and 51, 7 times; then repeat Row 50 once **more**: 33 dc.

Row 67: Ch 2, turn; work beginning decrease, dc in next dc and in each dc across, ch 50 (tie); finish off: 32 dc and one tie.

Row 68: With **right** side facing, skip tie and join yarn with dc in first dc; dc in next dc and in each dc across to last 2 dc, decrease: 31 dc.

Rows 69-95: Repeat Rows 50 and 51, 13 times; then repeat Row 50 once **more**: 4 dc.

Row 96: Ch 2, turn; dc in first 2 dc, decrease: 3 dc.

Row 97: Ch 2, turn; work beginning decrease, dc in last dc: 2 dc.

Row 98: Ch 2, turn; dc in first 2 dc; finish off.

Holding 2 strands of yarn together, each 18" (45.5 cm) long, add fringe in end of each row across increase/decrease edge ***(Figs. 8c & d, page 12)***.

NOT-SO-GRANNY SQUARE WRAP

Shown on page 6.

INTERMEDIATE

Finished Size: Adult

MATERIALS

BULKY 5

Bulky Weight Yarn [6 ounces, 185 yards (170 grams, 167 meters) per skein]:
- Main Color (Dk Grey) - One skein
- Assorted scrap colors (minimum of 6 colors) 435 yards (398 meters)

Crochet hook, size K (6.5 mm) **or** size needed for gauge
Yarn needle

GAUGE: 9 dc and 6 rounds = 4" (10 cm)
One Square = $10^{1}/_{2}$" (26.5 cm)

Gauge Swatch: $3^{1}/_{2}$" (9 cm) square
Work same as Square through Rnd 2.

STITCH GUIDE

DECREASE (uses next 2 dc)
★ YO, insert hook in **next** dc, YO and pull up a loop, YO and draw through 2 loops on hook; repeat from ★ once **more**, YO and draw through all 3 loops on hook **(counts as one dc)**.

SQUARE (Make 6)

There are 7 rounds to each Square, each round being worked with a different color. Choose your own color sequence or change colors randomly. Use Main Color for the 7th round of each Square. Listed below is the approximately yardage/meters it takes to work each round.

	Yards	Meters
Rnd 1	4	3.5
Rnd 2	6	5.5
Rnd 3	8	7.5
Rnd 4	10	9
Rnd 5	12	11
Rnd 6	14	13
Rnd 7	16	14.5

With first color, ch 4; join with slip st to form a ring.

Rnd 1: Ch 3 **(counts as first dc, now and throughout)**, 2 dc in ring, (ch 2, 3 dc in ring) 3 times, hdc in first dc to form last ch-2 sp changing to desired color ***(Fig. 7a, page 12)***: 12 dc and 4 ch-2 sps.

Rnd 2 (Right side)**:** Ch 3, turn; 2 dc in last ch-2 sp made, ch 1, ★ (3 dc, ch 2, 3 dc) in next ch-2 sp, ch 1; repeat from ★ 2 times **more**, 3 dc in same sp as first dc, hdc in first dc to form last ch-2 sp changing to desired color: 24 dc and 8 sps.

Note: Loop a short piece of yarn around any stitch to mark Rnd 2 as **right** side.

Instructions continued on page 4.

Rnd 3: Ch 3, turn; 2 dc in last ch-2 sp made, ch 1, 3 dc in next ch-1 sp, ch 1, ★ (3 dc, ch 2, 3 dc) in next ch-2 sp, ch 1, 3 dc in next ch-1 sp, ch 1; repeat from ★ 2 times **more**, 3 dc in same sp as first dc, hdc in first dc to form last ch-2 sp changing to desired color: 36 dc and 12 sps.

Rnd 4: Ch 3, turn; 2 dc in last ch-2 sp made, ch 1, (3 dc in next ch-1 sp, ch 1) twice, ★ (3 dc, ch 2, 3 dc) in next ch-2 sp, ch 1, (3 dc in next ch-1 sp, ch 1) twice; repeat from ★ 2 times **more**, 3 dc in same sp as first dc, hdc in first dc to form last ch-2 sp changing to desired color: 48 dc and 16 sps.

Rnd 5: Ch 3, turn; 2 dc in last ch-2 sp made, ch 1, (3 dc in next ch-1 sp, ch 1) 3 times, ★ (3 dc, ch 2, 3 dc) in next ch-2 sp, ch 1, (3 dc in next ch-1 sp, ch 1) 3 times; repeat from ★ 2 times **more**, 3 dc in same sp as first dc, hdc in first dc to form last ch-2 sp changing to desired color: 60 dc and 20 sps.

Rnd 6: Ch 3, turn; 2 dc in last ch-2 sp made, ch 1, (3 dc in next ch-1 sp, ch 1) 4 times, ★ (3 dc, ch 2, 3 dc) in next ch-2 sp, ch 1, (3 dc in next ch-1 sp, ch 1) 4 times; repeat from ★ 2 times **more**, 3 dc in same sp as first dc, hdc in first dc to form last ch-2 sp changing to Main Color: 72 dc and 24 sps.

Rnd 7: Ch 3, turn; 2 dc in last ch-2 sp made, ch 1, (3 dc in next ch-1 sp, ch 1) 5 times, ★ (3 dc, ch 2, 3 dc) in next ch-2 sp, ch 1, (3 dc in next ch-1 sp, ch 1) 5 times; repeat from ★ 2 times **more**, 3 dc in same sp as first dc, ch 2; join with slip st to first dc, finish off leaving a long end for sewing: 84 dc and 28 sps.

ASSEMBLY

Place two Squares with **wrong** sides together. Thread yarn needle with long end of Main Color and beginning in second ch of first corner, sew through both pieces once to secure the beginning of the seam. Insert the needle from **front** to **back** through **both** loops of each stitch on **both** pieces ***(Fig. A)***. Bring needle around and insert it from **front** to **back** through next loops of both pieces. Continue in this manner across to first ch of next corner, keeping sewing yarn fairly loose.

Fig. A

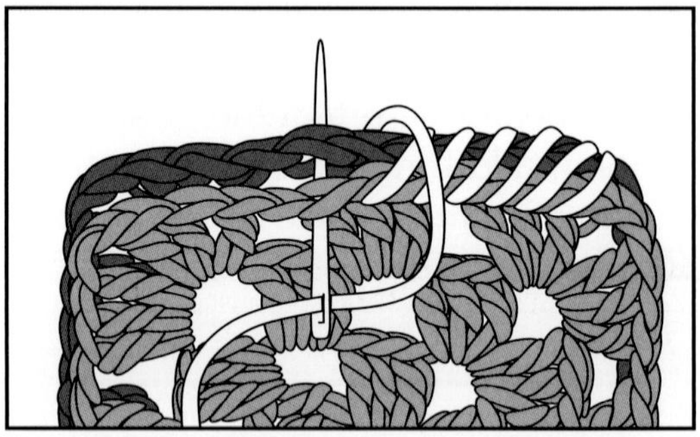

Using Placement Diagram as a guide, sew a third Square to previous two Squares to form a V shape. Repeat with remaining 3 Squares.

PLACEMENT DIAGRAM

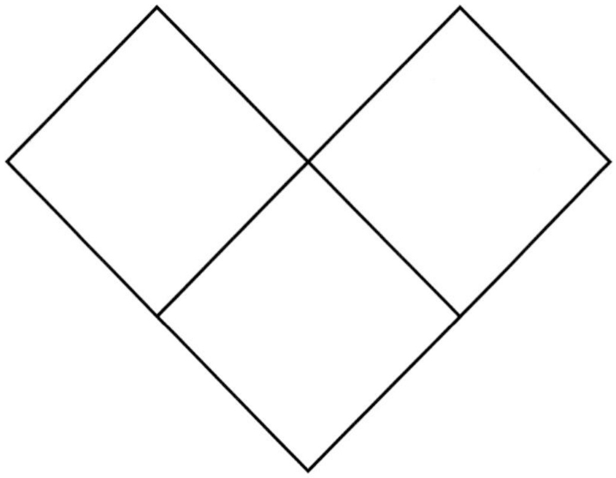

With **wrong** sides of V shapes together, sew pieces together in same manner to form shoulder seams.

NECKLINE

There are 8 rounds for the Neckline, each round being worked with a different color. Choose your own color sequence or change colors randomly. Use Main Color for the 1st and 8th round of the Neckline. Listed below is the approximately yardage/meters it takes to work each round.

	Yards	Meters
Rnd 1	15	13.5
Rnd 2	15	13.5
Rnd 3	15	13.5
Rnd 4	14	13
Rnd 5	13	12
Rnd 6	13	12
Rnd 7	13	12

Rnd 1: With **right** side facing, join Main Color with dc in either shoulder seam ***(see Joining With Dc, page 12)***; dc in next 21 dc and in next 2 ch-2 sps, dc in next 21 dc and in next shoulder seam, dc in next 21 dc and in next 2 ch-2 sps, dc in last 21 dc; join with slip st to first dc changing to desired color ***(Fig. 7b, page 12)***: 90 dc.

Rnd 2: Ch 3, turn; dc in next 20 dc, decrease twice, dc in next 41 dc, decrease twice, dc in last 20 dc; join with slip st to first dc changing to desired color: 86 dc.

Rnd 3: Ch 3, turn; dc in next 19 dc, decrease twice, dc in next 39 dc, decrease twice, dc in last 19 dc; join with slip st to first dc changing to desired color: 82 dc.

Rnd 4: Ch 3, turn; dc in next 18 dc, decrease twice, dc in next 37 dc, decrease twice, dc in last 18 dc; join with slip st to first dc changing to desired color: 78 dc.

Rnd 5: Ch 3, turn; dc in next 17 dc, decrease twice, dc in next 35 dc, decrease twice, dc in last 17 dc; join with slip st to first dc changing to desired color: 74 dc.

Rnd 6: Ch 3, turn; dc in next 16 dc, decrease twice, dc in next 33 dc, decrease twice, dc in last 16 dc; join with slip st to first dc changing to desired color: 70 dc.

Rnd 7: Ch 3, turn; dc in next 15 dc, decrease twice, dc in next 31 dc, decrease twice, dc in last 15 dc; join with slip st to first dc changing to Main Color: 66 dc.

Rnd 8: Ch 3, turn; dc in next 14 dc, decrease twice, dc in next 29 dc, decrease twice, dc in last 14 dc; join with slip st to first dc, finish off.

BOTTOM EDGING

With **right** side facing, join Main Color with dc in ch-2 sp of any bottom point; (dc, ch 2, 2 dc) in same sp, ch 1, (dc, ch 1) in each dc and in each joining across to next ch-2 sp, (2 dc, ch 2, 2 dc) in ch-2 sp, ch 1, (dc, ch 1) in each dc and in each joining across; join with slip st to first dc, finish off.

Holding 2 strands of desired color together, each 18" (45.5 cm) long, add fringe in each sp around Bottom Edging ***(Figs. 8a & b, page 12)***.

BUTTERFLY WRAP

Shown on page 7.

INTERMEDIATE

Finished Size: Adult

MATERIALS

BULKY 5

Bulky Weight Yarn
[6 ounces, 185 yards
(170 grams, 167 meters) per skein]:
3 skeins
Crochet hook, size K (6.5 mm) **or** size needed for gauge

GAUGE: 9 dc and 6 rows = 4" (10 cm)

Gauge Swatch: 7" x $5^1/_4$" x $5^1/_4$"
(17.75 cm x 13.25 cm x 13.25 cm)
Work same as Wrap through Row 3.

WRAP

Beginning at back neck edge, ch 4; join with slip st to form a ring.

Row 1 (Right side)**:** Ch 3 **(counts as first dc, now and throughout)**, (3 dc, ch 2, 4 dc) in ring: 8 dc and one ch-2 sp.

Note: Loop a short piece of yarn around any stitch to mark Row 1 as **right** side.

Row 2: Ch 3, turn; dc in same st and in next 3 dc, (2 dc, ch 2, 2 dc) in next ch-2 sp, dc in next 3 dc, 2 dc in last dc: 14 dc and one ch-2 sp.

Row 3: Ch 3, turn; dc in same st and in next 6 dc, (2 dc, ch 2, 2 dc) in next ch-2 sp, dc in next 6 dc, 2 dc in last dc: 20 dc and one ch-2 sp.

Row 4: Ch 3, turn; dc in same st, ch 1, skip next dc, (dc in next dc, ch 1, skip next dc) 4 times, (2 dc, ch 2, 2 dc) in next ch-2 sp, ch 1, skip next dc, (dc in next dc, ch 1, skip next dc) 4 times, 2 dc in last dc: 16 dc and 11 sps.

Row 5: Ch 3, turn; dc in same st and in each dc and each ch-1 sp across to next ch-2 sp, (2 dc, ch 2, 2 dc) in ch-2 sp, dc in next dc and in each dc and each ch-1 sp across to last dc, 2 dc in last dc: 32 dc and one ch-2 sp.

Rows 6 and 7: Ch 3, turn; dc in same st and in each dc across to next ch-2 sp, (2 dc, ch 2, 2 dc) in ch-2 sp, dc in next dc and in each dc across to last dc, 2 dc in last dc: 44 dc and one ch-2 sp.

Row 8: Ch 3, turn; dc in same st, ch 1, skip next dc, (dc in next dc, ch 1, skip next dc) 10 times, (2 dc, ch 2, 2 dc) in next ch-2 sp, ch 1, skip next dc, (dc in next dc, ch 1, skip next dc) 10 times, 2 dc in last dc: 28 dc and 23 sps.

Row 9: Ch 3, turn; dc in same st and in each dc and each ch-1 sp across to next ch-2 sp, (2 dc, ch 2, 2 dc) in ch-2 sp, dc in next dc and in each dc and each ch-1 sp across to last dc, 2 dc in last dc: 56 dc and one ch-2 sp.

Row 10: Ch 3, turn; dc in same st and in next 12 dc, (dc, ch 2, dc) in next dc, dc in next 14 dc, (2 dc, ch 2, 2 dc) in next ch-2 sp, dc in next 14 dc, (dc, ch 2, dc) in next dc, dc in next 12 dc, 2 dc in last dc: 64 dc and 3 ch-2 sps.

Row 11: Ch 3, turn; dc in same st and in next 14 dc, (dc, ch 2, dc) in next ch-2 sp, dc in next 17 dc, (2 dc, ch 2, 2 dc) in next ch-2 sp, dc in next 17 dc, (dc, ch 2, dc) in next ch-2 sp, dc in next 14 dc, 2 dc in last dc: 74 dc and 3 ch-2 sps.

Row 12: Ch 3, turn; dc in same st, (ch 1, skip next dc, dc in next dc) 8 times, (dc, ch 2, dc) in next ch-2 sp, (dc in next dc, ch 1, skip next dc) 10 times, (2 dc, ch 2, 2 dc) in next ch-2 sp, (ch 1, skip next dc, dc in next dc) 10 times, (dc, ch 2, dc) in next ch-2 sp, (dc in next dc, ch 1, skip next dc) 8 times, 2 dc in last dc: 48 dc and 39 sps.

Row 13: Ch 3, turn; dc in same st and in each dc and each ch-1 sp across to next ch-2 sp, (dc, ch 2, dc) in ch-2 sp, dc in next dc and in each dc and each ch-1 sp across to next ch-2 sp, (2 dc, ch 2, 2 dc) in ch-2 sp, dc in next dc and in each dc and each ch-1 sp across to next ch-2 sp, (dc, ch 2, dc) in ch-2 sp, dc in next dc and in each dc and each ch-1 sp across to last dc, 2 dc in last dc; finish off: 94 dc and 3 ch-2 sps.

Row 14: Ch 50 (tie); with **wrong** side facing, join yarn with dc in first dc ***(see Joining With Dc, page 12)***; dc in same st and in each dc across to next ch-2 sp, (dc, ch 2, dc) in ch-2 sp, dc in next dc and in each dc across to next ch-2 sp, (2 dc, ch 2, 2 dc) in ch-2 sp, dc in next dc and in each dc across to next ch-2 sp, (dc, ch 2, dc) in ch-2 sp, dc in next dc and in each dc across to last dc, 2 dc in last dc, ch 50 (tie); finish off: 104 dc, 3 ch-2 sps, and 2 ties.

Row 15: With **right** side facing, join yarn with dc in first dc; dc in same st and in each dc across to next ch-2 sp, (dc, ch 2, dc) in ch-2 sp, dc in next dc and in each dc across to next ch-2 sp, (2 dc, ch 2, 2 dc) in ch-2 sp, dc in next dc and in each dc across to next ch-2 sp, (dc, ch 2, dc) in ch-2 sp, dc in next dc and in each dc across to last dc, 2 dc in last dc: 114 dc and 3 ch-2 sps.

Rows 16-18: Ch 3, turn; dc in same st and in each dc across to next ch-2 sp, (dc, ch 2, dc) in ch-2 sp, dc in next dc and in each dc across to next ch-2 sp, (2 dc, ch 2, 2 dc) in ch-2 sp, dc in next dc and in each dc across to next ch-2 sp, (dc, ch 2, dc) in ch-2 sp, dc in next dc and in each dc across to last dc, 2 dc in last dc: 144 dc and 3 ch-2 sps.

Row 19: Ch 3, turn; dc in same st, (ch 1, skip next dc, dc in next dc) 15 times, (dc, ch 2, dc) in next ch-2 sp, dc in next dc, (ch 1, skip next dc, dc in next dc) 20 times, (2 dc, ch 2, 2 dc) in next ch-2 sp, dc in next dc, (ch 1, skip next dc, dc in next dc) 20 times, (dc, ch 2, dc) in next ch-2 sp, (dc in next dc, ch 1, skip next dc) 15 times, 2 dc in last dc: 84 dc and 73 sps.

Row 20: Ch 3, turn; dc in same st and in each dc and each ch-1 sp across to next ch-2 sp, (dc, ch 2, dc) in ch-2 sp, dc in next dc and in each dc and each ch-1 sp across to next ch-2 sp, (2 dc, ch 2, 2 dc) in ch-2 sp, dc in next dc and in each dc and each ch-1 sp across to next ch-2 sp, (dc, ch 2, dc) in ch-2 sp, dc in next dc and in each dc and each ch-1 sp across to last dc, 2 dc in last dc: 164 dc and 3 ch-2 sps.

Rows 21-24: Ch 3, turn; dc in same st and in each dc across to next ch-2 sp, (dc, ch 2, dc) in ch-2 sp, dc in next dc and in each dc across to next ch-2 sp, (2 dc, ch 2, 2 dc) in ch-2 sp, dc in next dc and in each dc across to next ch-2 sp, (dc, ch 2, dc) in ch-2 sp, dc in next dc and in each dc across to last dc, 2 dc in last dc: 204 dc and 3 ch-2 sps.

Row 25: Ch 3, turn; 4 dc in same st, (skip next 2 dc, sc in next dc, skip next 2 dc, 5 dc in next dc) 7 times, sc in next ch-2 sp, 5 dc in next dc, skip next 2 dc, sc in next dc, (skip next 2 dc, 5 dc in next dc, skip next 2 dc, sc in next dc) 9 times, skip next dc, 5 dc in next ch-2 sp, skip next dc, sc in next dc, skip next 2 dc, 5 dc in next dc, (skip next 2 dc, sc in next dc, skip next 2 dc, 5 dc in next dc) 9 times, sc in next ch-2 sp, 5 dc in next dc, (skip next 2 dc, sc in next dc, skip next 2 dc, 5 dc in next dc) 7 times; finish off.

GENERAL INSTRUCTIONS

ABBREVIATIONS

ch(s)	chain(s)
cm	centimeters
hdc	half double crochet(s)
dc	double crochet(s)
mm	millimeters
Rnd(s)	Rounds
sc	single crochet(s)
sp(s)	space(s)
st(s)	stitch(es)
YO	yarn over

★ — work instructions following ★ as many **more** times as indicated in addition to the first time.

( ) or **[ ]** — work enclosed instructions **as many** times as specified by the number immediately following **or** work all enclosed instructions in the stitch or space indicated **or** contains explanatory remarks.

colon (:) — the number(s) given after a colon at the end of a row or round denote(s) the number of stitches or spaces you should have on that row or round.

CROCHET TERMINOLOGY		
UNITED STATES		**INTERNATIONAL**
slip stitch (slip st)	=	single crochet (sc)
single crochet (sc)	=	double crochet (dc)
half double crochet (hdc)	=	half treble crochet (htr)
double crochet (dc)	=	treble crochet (tr)
treble crochet (tr)	=	double treble crochet (dtr)
double treble crochet (dtr)	=	triple treble crochet (ttr)
triple treble crochet (tr tr)	=	quadruple treble crochet (qtr)
skip	=	miss

GAUGE

Exact gauge is **essential** for proper fit. Before beginning your project, make the sample swatch given in the individual instructions in the yarn and hook specified. After completing the swatch, measure it, counting your stitches and rows/rounds carefully. If your swatch is larger or smaller than specified, **make another, changing hook size to get the correct gauge**. Keep trying until you find the size hook that will give you the specified gauge. Once proper gauge is obtained, measure width of garment approximately every 3" (7.5 cm) to be sure gauge remains consistent.

Yarn Weight Symbol & Names	SUPER FINE 1	FINE 2	LIGHT 3	MEDIUM 4	BULKY 5	SUPER BULKY 6
Type of Yarns in Category	Sock, Fingering Baby	Sport, Baby	DK, Light Worsted	Worsted, Afghan, Aran	Chunky, Craft, Rug	Bulky, Roving
Crochet Gauge Ranges in Single Crochet to 4" (10 cm)	21-32 sts	16-20 sts	12-17 sts	11-14 sts	8-11 sts	5-9 sts
Advised Hook Size Range	B-1 to E-4	E-4 to 7	7 to I-9	I-9 to K-10.5	K-10.5 to M-13	M-13 and larger

ALUMINUM CROCHET HOOKS													
U.S.	B-1	C-2	D-3	E-4	F-5	G-6	H-8	I-9	J-10	K-10½	N	P	Q
Metric - mm	2.25	2.75	3.25	3.5	3.75	4	5	5.5	6	6.5	9	10	15

BEGINNER	Projects for first-time crocheters using basic stitches. Minimal shaping.
EASY	Projects using yarn with basic stitches, repetitive stitch patterns, simple color changes, and simple shaping and finishing.
INTERMEDIATE	Projects using a variety of techniques, such as basic lace patterns or color patterns, mid-level shaping and finishing.
EXPERIENCED	Projects with intricate stitch patterns, techniques and dimension, such as non-repeating patterns, multi-color techniques, fine threads, small hooks, detailed shaping and refined finishing.

CHAIN

To work a chain stitch, begin with a slip knot on the hook. Bring the yarn **over** hook from back to front, catching the yarn with the hook and turning the hook slightly toward you to keep the yarn from slipping off. Draw the yarn through the slip knot ***(Fig. 1)*** **(first chain stitch made, *abbreviated ch*)**.

Fig. 1

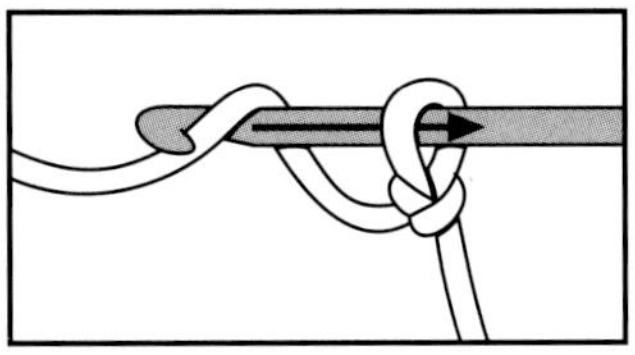

WORKING INTO THE CHAIN

When counting chains, always begin with the first chain from the hook and then count toward the beginning of your foundation chain ***(Fig. 2a)***.

Fig. 2a

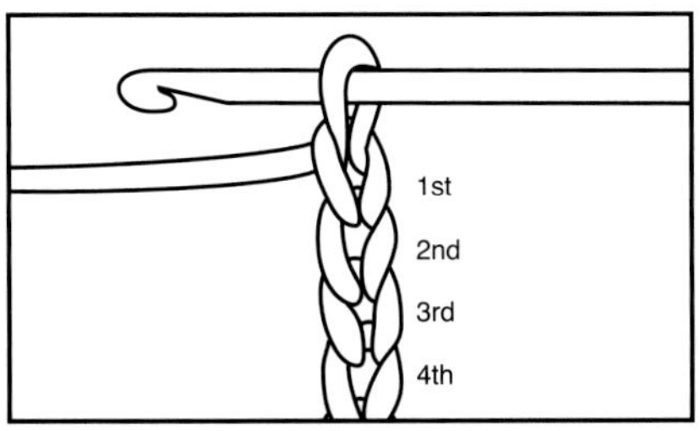

Method 1: Insert hook into back ridge of each chain ***(Fig. 2b)***.

Method 2: Insert hook under top two strands of each chain ***(Fig. 2c)***.

Fig. 2b

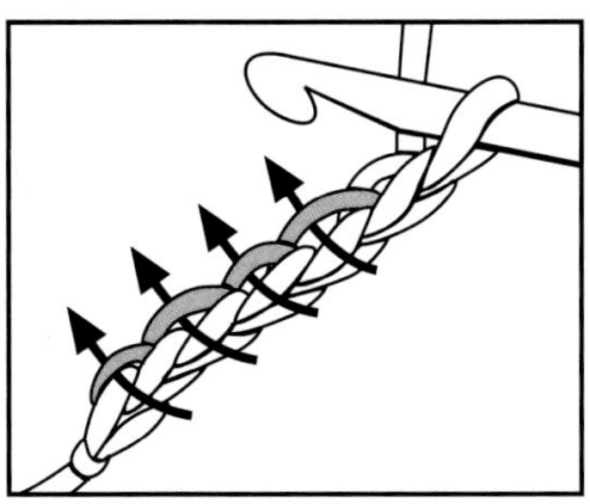

Fig. 2c

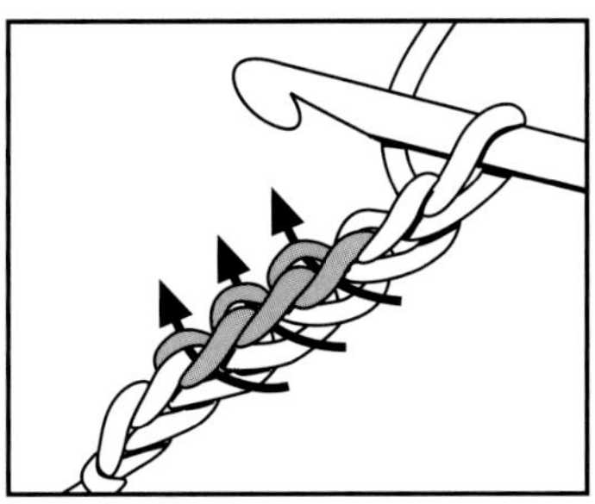

Method 3: To form a beginning ring, work the specified number of chains and then join to the first chain made with a slip stitch ***(Fig. 2d)***.

Fig. 2d

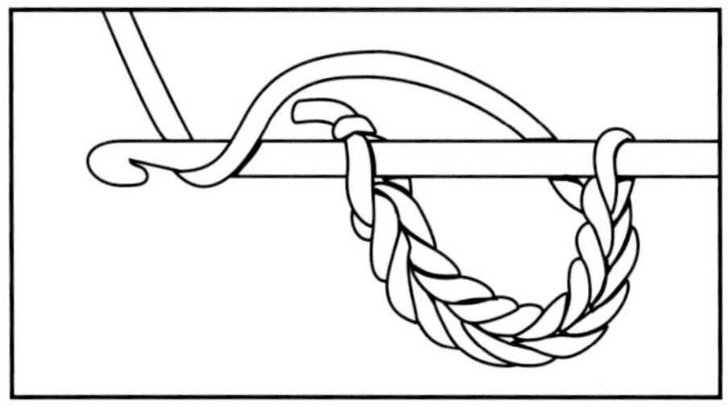

SLIP STITCH

To work a slip stitch, insert hook in stitch or space indicated, YO and draw through stitch and through loop on hook ***(Fig. 3)*** **(slip stitch made, *abbreviated slip st*)**.

Fig. 3

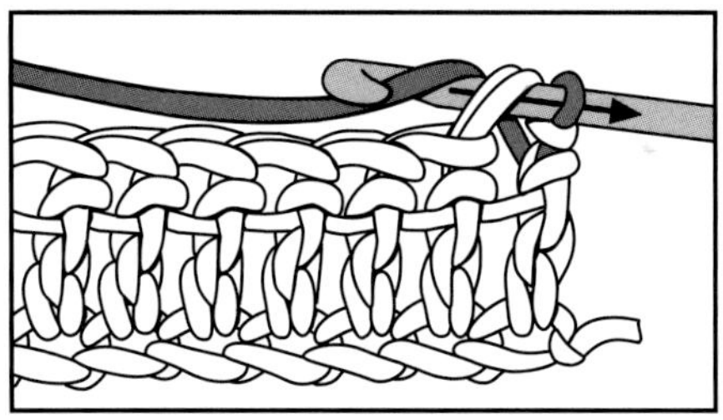

SINGLE CROCHET

Insert hook in stitch or space indicated, YO and pull up a loop, YO and draw through both loops on hook ***(Fig. 4)*** **(single crochet made, *abbreviated sc*)**.

Fig. 4

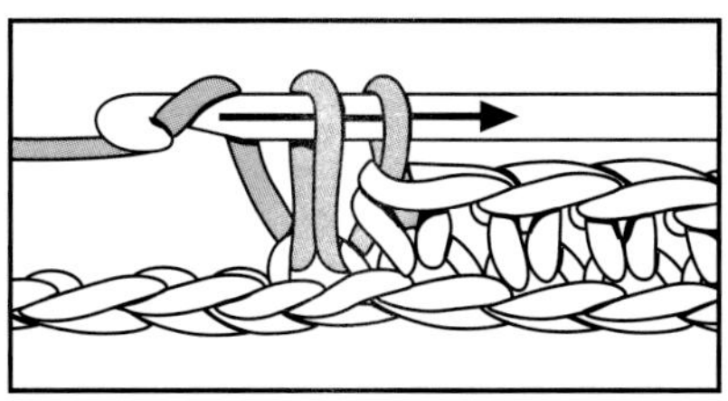

HALF DOUBLE CROCHET

YO, insert hook in stitch or space indicated, YO and pull up a loop, YO and draw through all 3 loops on hook ***(Fig. 5)*** **(half double crochet made, *abbreviated hdc*)**.

Fig. 5

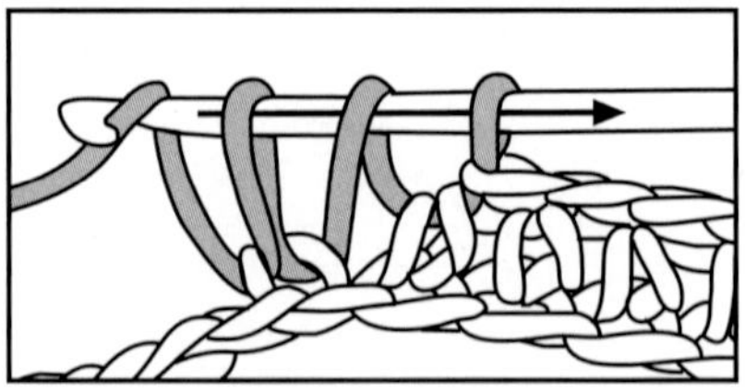

DOUBLE CROCHET

YO, insert hook in stitch or space indicated, YO and pull up a loop (3 loops on hook), YO and draw through 2 loops on hook ***(Fig. 6a)***, YO and draw through remaining 2 loops on hook ***(Fig. 6b)*** **(double crochet made, *abbreviated dc*)**.

Fig. 6a

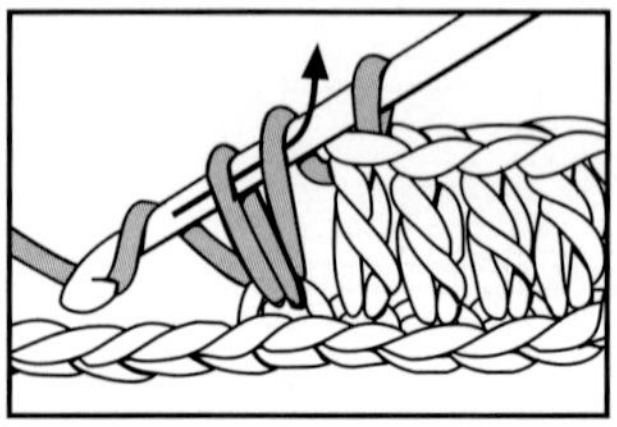

Fig. 6b

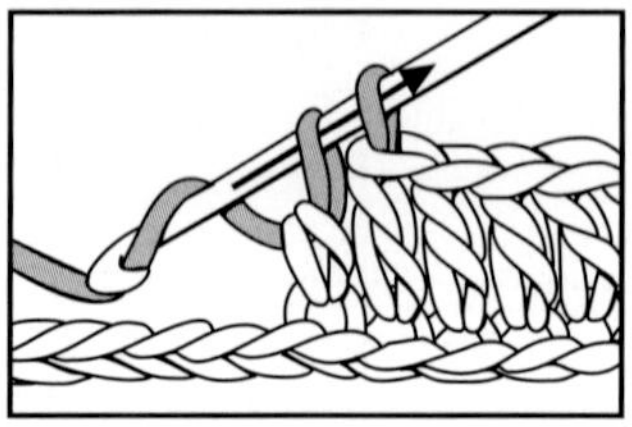

CHANGING COLORS

To change colors in last st made, insert hook in stitch indicated, YO and pull up a loop, drop yarn, with new yarn ***(Fig. 7a)***, YO and draw through all loops on hook.

To change colors at the end of a round by joining with a slip st, drop yarn, insert hook in first stitch of round, holding new yarn, YO and draw through stitch and loop on hook ***(Fig. 7b)***.

Fig. 7a

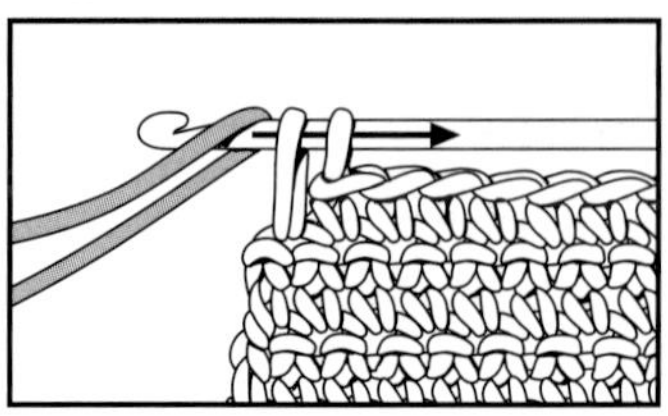

Fig. 7b

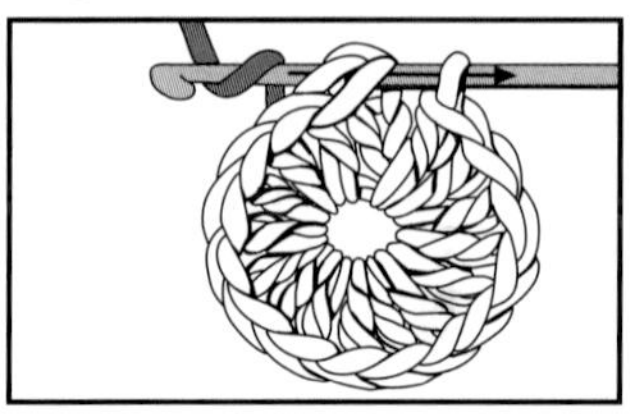

JOINING WITH DC

When instructed to join with dc, begin with a slip knot on hook. YO, holding loop on hook, insert hook in stitch or space indicated, YO and pull up a loop (3 loops on hook), (YO and draw through 2 loops on hook) twice.

FRINGE

Cut a piece of cardboard 8" (20.5 cm) wide and half as long as strands indicated in individual instructions. Wind the yarn **loosely** and **evenly** lengthwise around the cardboard until the card is filled, then cut across one end; repeat as needed.

Hold together as many strands of yarn as specified in individual instructions; fold in half.

With **wrong** side facing and using a crochet hook, draw the folded end up through a space, stitch or row and pull the loose ends through the folded end ***(Figs. 8a & c)***; draw the knot up tightly ***(Figs. 8b & d)***. Repeat spacing as specified in individual instructions.

Lay flat on a hard surface and trim the ends.

Fig. 8a

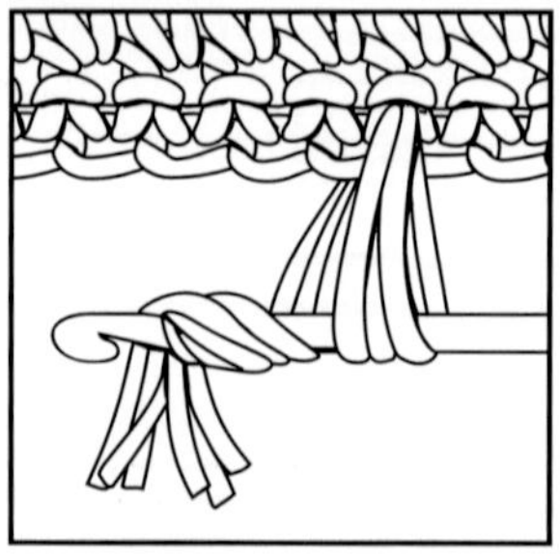

Fig. 8b

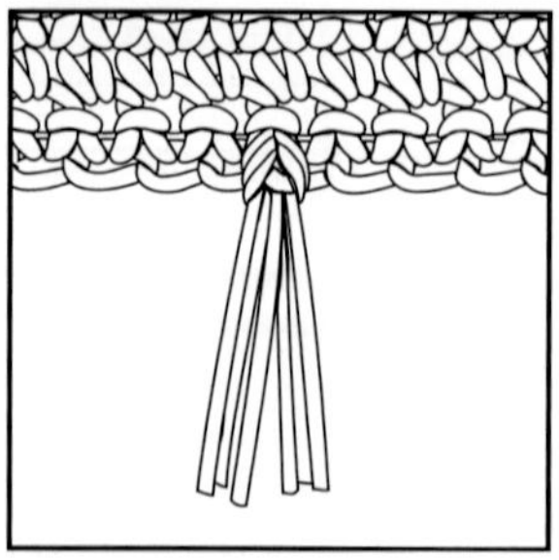

Fig. 8c

Fig. 8d

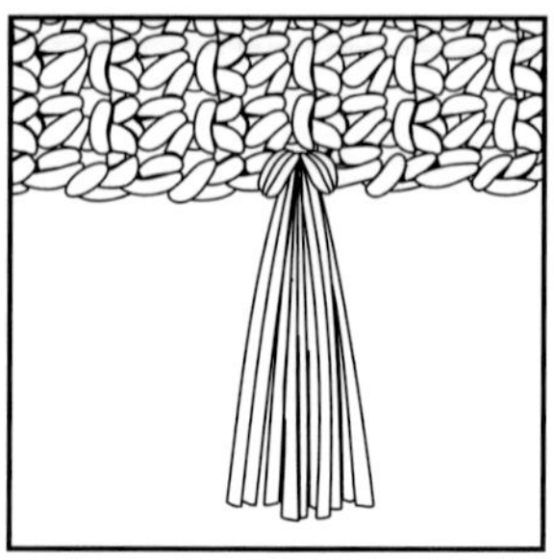